# Water
# Detective

Carol Alexander
Photography by Bill Burlingham

Emily's class was having a science fair. "Everyone should think of a project," Ms. Turner said. "We've studied water, animals, and plants. Choose a topic."

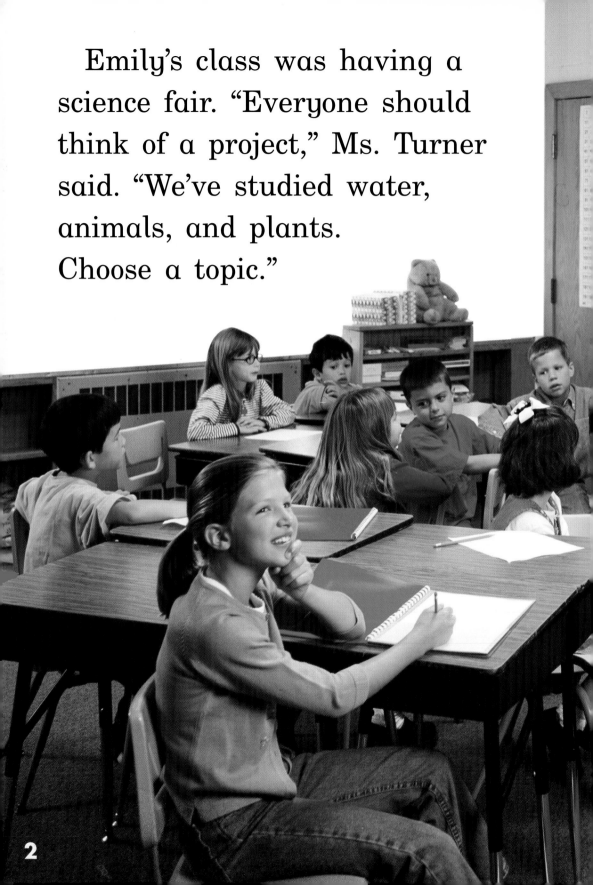

5 Pretend you're playing "Guess the Covered Word"
south
Water
Animals
Plants
Olivia Armstrong
Jesse Conterato
Mallory Corrus
Teddy Gabrielides
Keri Golembeski
Joanie Guidarelli
Sam Hersh
Sam Rodman
Henry Lee
Hannah Litvan
Joaquín Montoya
Max Perkins
Billy Rivi
Emily O'Brien
Drew Sillars
Madeleine Tirva
Claire Dechamps
Jack Weisenberger
Caroline Wright
Kristen Yang
Meredith Stock

Emily decided to do her project on saving water. She wanted to be a Water Detective! She listed things to investigate in her journal. To show she was serious, she wore a badge and made awards to hand out. She read information in library books.

Water Detective

Water Saver

**What I Know**
- There is not enough water on Earth for all our needs.
- People waste a lot of water.

**What I Want to Learn**
- How do we waste water?
- What can we do to stop wasting water?

**How to Find Out More**
- Get books from the library.
- Observe the ways my family uses water.

## Monday, March 4

Today Mom left the water running while she was washing the car. I told her to use a bucket instead.

Now Mom turns on the water only when she needs it. I gave Mom an award! Good job, Mom!

## Tuesday, March 5

I caught Dad leaving the water running while he rinsed the dishes. I told him to rinse the dishes in a tub instead.

So Dad filled the tub with rinse water and turned off the faucet. We are a great team!

## Wednesday, March 6

I learned this from a book.

- A big milk jug holds 1 gallon.
- Every minute the faucet is on, about 4 gallons of water are used.

One
Gallon

I decided to turn off the water while I brush my teeth. This chart shows how much water I save. I gave myself a Water Saver award!

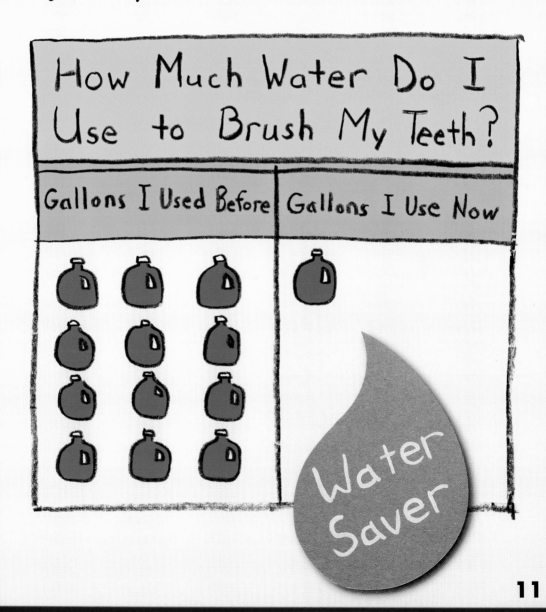

| How Much Water Do I Use to Brush My Teeth? | |
|---|---|
| Gallons I Used Before | Gallons I Use Now |

Water Saver

## Thursday, March 7

This morning my brother was brushing his teeth. That's the good news. The bad news is that he left the water running! I told him to turn off the water and fill a cup to rinse his mouth.

Now he turns off the water.

I gave him a Water Saver award.

I think it went to his head!

# Friday, March 8

Today I noticed a leaky faucet. The Water Detective is on the job!

I showed the leak to Mom and she fixed it. Mom said, "Good work, Detective H$_2$O!" She told me that H$_2$O is what scientists call water.

## Monday, March 11

I read that bricks in the toilet tank save water. I did an experiment. I took two buckets. I put some bricks in one bucket. Then I filled both buckets with water. It took less water to fill the bucket with the bricks!

So Dad put some bricks in our toilet tank. Now it uses less water to fill. We save water every time we flush!

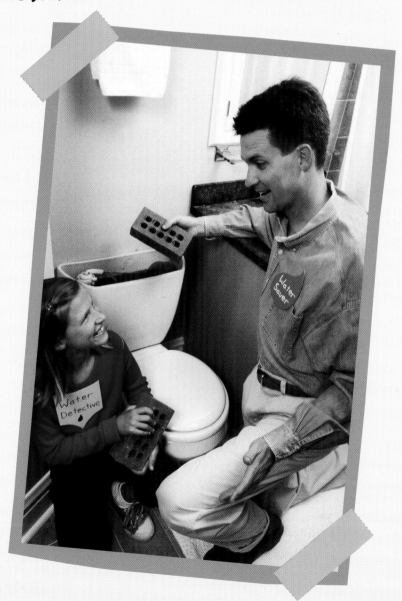

## Tuesday, March 12

I also read about a special showerhead that saves water.

This chart shows how much water the special showerhead uses.

# Wednesday, March 13

When I showed Dad my chart, he was impressed. We bought the special showerhead.

Dad put on the showerhead right away. He was proud of me for saving water!

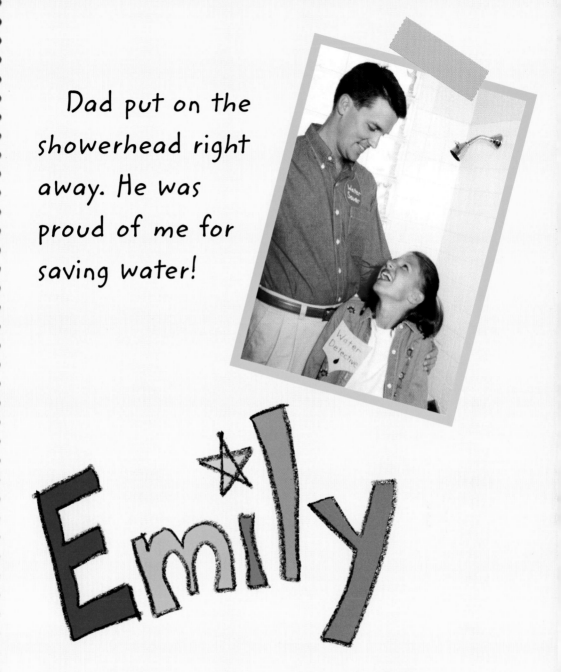

Emily

P. S. This is my last journal entry because tomorrow I need to make my poster. Wish me luck!

Finally the day of the science fair arrived. Everyone was excited about their projects. Emily told about her work as Detective $H_2O$. She handed out a list of water-saving tips.

# What I Learned

This Is What I Learned:

1. Every minute a faucet is left on, about four gallons of water are used. That's a lot of water!

2. You can save 11 gallons of water each time you brush your teeth by turning off the water.

3. You can save a gallon of water each time you flush if you put four bricks in your toilet tank.

4. If you use a special water saving shower head, you can save three gallons of water a minute.

Emily blushed when Ms. Turner gave her a ribbon for her project! She had learned a lot about saving water.

If you leave the water running, watch out for the Water Detective!